POETRY FROM CRESCENT MOON

William Shakespeare: *Selected Sonnets and Verse*
edited, with an introduction by Mark Tuley

William Shakespeare: *The Sonnets*
edited and introduced by Mark Tuley

*Shakespeare: Love, Poetry and Magic
in Shakespeare's Sonnets and Plays*
by B.D. Barnacle

Edmund Spenser: *Heavenly Love: Selected Poems*
selected and introduced by Teresa Page

Robert Herrick: *Delight In Disorder: Selected Poems*
edited and introduced by M.K. Pace

Sir Thomas Wyatt: *Love For Love: Selected Poems*
selected and introduced by Louise Cooper

John Donne: *Air and Angels: Selected Poems*
selected and introduced by A.H. Ninham

D.H. Lawrence: *Being Alive: Selected Poems*
edited with an introduction by Margaret Elvy

D.H. Lawrence: Symbolic Landscapes
by Jane Foster

D.H. Lawrence: Infinite Sensual Violence
by M.K. Pace

Percy Bysshe Shelley: *Paradise of Golden Lights: Selected Poems*
selected and introduced by Charlotte Greene

Thomas Hardy: *Her Haunting Ground: Selected Poems*
edited, with an introduction by A.H. Ninham

Sexing Hardy: Thomas Hardy and Feminism
by Margaret Elvy

Emily Bronte: *Darkness and Glory: Selected Poems*
selected and introduced by Miriam Chalk

John Keats: *Bright Star: Selected Poems*
edited with an introduction by Miriam Chalk

Arthur Rimbaud: *A Season in Hell*
edited and translated by Andrew Jary

Rimbaud: Arthur Rimbaud and the Magic of Poetry
by Jeremy Mark Robinson

Friedrich Hölderlin: *Hölderlin's Songs of Light: Selected Poems*
translated by Michael Hamburger

Rainer Maria Rilke: *Dance the Orange:* Selected Poems
translated by Michael Hamburger

Rilke: Space, Essence and Angels in the Poetry of Rainer Maria Rilke
by B.D. Barnacle

German Romantic Poetry: Goethe, Novalis,
Heine, Hölderlin, Schlegel, Schiller
by Carol Appleby

Arseny Tarkovsky: *Life, Life: Selected Poems*
translated by Virginia Rounding

Emily Dickinson: *Wild Nights: Selected Poems*
selected and introduced by Miriam Chalk

Cavafy: Anatomy of a Soul
by Matt Crispin

D.J. ENRIGHT

Born in 1920, D.J. Enright has written numerous books, including *Instant Chronicles: A Life* (Oxford University Press, 1985), *The Alluring Problem: An Essay On Irony* (OUP, 1986), *Fields of Vision* (OUP, 1988), *Under the Circumstances* (OUP, 1991) and *Old Men and Comets* (OUP, 1993). He has edited three Oxford books: *The Oxford Book of Death*, *The Oxford Book of Contemporary Verse* and *The Oxford Book of Friendship*. He has also edited *Fair of Speech* (1985) and *The Faber Book of Fevers and Frets* (1989).

Earlier books include *The Laughing Hyena* (1953), *Literature For Man's Sake* (1955), *Bread Rather Than Blossom* (1956), *Insufficient Poppy* (1960), *Conspirators and Poets* (1966), *Shakespeare and the Students* (1970), and *A Faust Book* (1979). Enright received the Queen's Gold Medal for Poetry in 1981.

Of D.J. Enright's 1987 *Collected Poems* (OUP), Gavin Ewart wrote in *The Observer*: 'Anybody at all interested in English poetry should read this book. It has in it the best autobiographic sequence written this century... It also contains some of the wittiest and wryest comment on the modern world to be written in our time.'

By-Blows

By-Blows
Uncollected Poems

D.J. ENRIGHT

CRESCENT MOON

Crescent Moon Publishing
P.O. Box 393
Maidstone
Kent
ME14 5XU, U.K.

First published 1996. Second edition 2008.
© D.J. Enright, 1996, 2008.

Printed and bound in Great Britain.
Set in Garamond 11 on 14pt.
Designed by Radiance Graphics.

British Library Cataloguing in Publication data

Enright, D.J., 1920-2002
By-Blows: Uncollected Poems - 2nd ed. (British Poets Series)
I. Title
821.9'14

ISBN 1-86171-150-6
ISBN-13 9781861711502

CONTENTS

ACKNOWLEDGEMENTS

Acknowledgements are due to the editors of the following periodicals, in which some of these poems first appeared; *Beloit Poetry Journal, Gown, Hubbub, London Magazine, London Review of Books, Passion, Rhinoceros, The Spectator, Thames Poetry* and *The Times Literary Supplement.*

WHITE NIGHTS

To make sure he slept with virgins only
He dispatched his loved ones in the morning,
For them there was no second coming.
Until one day there came a wiser maiden,
To tell him stories till the sun had risen.
It was tales the King was really keen on.
A thousand nights, at least a thousand,
The King forbore to kill the golden goose.
And when she finished her fabrications
(There were more, for sure, in reserve)
They felt themselves a staid old married couple.
Is this a mockery of matrimony,
A vile belittling of virginity,
A proleptic lesson in feminism,
Or a self-advertisement for fiction?
Hard to tell. Parables are always open
To a thousand morals and immorals.

WINDOW

When I was young his music was much loved –
A 'closet reactionary' they call him now.

All closets were reactionary when I was young,
And many were outside.
Outside my bedroom window
Stood the closet of The George in George Street,
Whether Saint or King I can't remember,
Stinking of reaction.

I never thought to link the two.
The music struck me as quite unlike
The closet.

Now, plagued by claustrophobia
And fear of crowds (however well dressed),
I give myself to closet Shakespeare.
Though smaller than the National Theatre,
My closet is less cluttered.

Solitary vices seize us in our childhood,
They enter through the bedroom window.

PETS

Research shows that keeping a cat
Helps you live longer.
You have to go out in the fresh air
To satisfy its hunger.

What other ways might help us?
Inside the hall a shotgun hidden,
Doors and letter-box sealed tight,
A sturdy shelter in the garden?

Nothing oncogenic in the larder,
Between your lips no cigarette,
Never hard stuff in the cellar,
Rarely a friendly body in your bed?

Better go out in the bracing air,
Hobble to the fishmonger,
The high streets stacked with tins,
To satisfy the creature's hunger.

•

There are no cats here, no pets,
As if they had all been eaten.
There were never any here to eat,
No one could afford to feed them.

Wild creatures prowl in the scrub,
On the outskirts of outskirts.

There is no such word as 'pet'.
Nothing lives long in these parts.

ANNIVERSARIES

Now it is fifteen/ twenty-five/ fifty years
    (*tick the applicable box*)
Since we were plundered/ raped/ tortured/ burned
Or otherwise maltreated
    (*ring the relevant entry*)
And again we are remembered,
And how we were starved, deported, shot down, gassed
Or otherwise.
Old newsreels flicker in hearths and homes
Where people are trying to eat their suppers
Or otherwise lead their largely innocuous lives
(Which their friends remember every twelvemonth).
Recalled at intervals of ten or fifty years,
Lest we should be forgotten.
For people need to remember,
Lest they forget what can always be done
In the way of
    (*fill in your preference*)
Since such things have happened before.

COLOUR SUPPLEMENTS

They cater for all of us
Here an individual in rags
There a display of the latest modes
Here an auto eats up the miles
There people drag through deserts
Here gilded youth is caught romping
There the elderly crouch in blankets
Here a shack of beaten petrol-cans
Over there a room of one's own
Here a whole tribe is hungry
Nearby are recipes for the gourmet –
No one at all need go without
Without being noticed on Sunday.

BUSY DAY

The poet at the Job Centre, looking for a challenging subject. 'Go out and live!' thunders the patriarchal manager, pointing to the door.

The poet at the Public Library, groaning over the papers: crime, passion, crimes of passion, disasters and horrors. 'Ssh!' hisses the peevish librarian, peering round the door.

The poet at the Building Society, murmuring of an ivory tower and the chances of a mortgage. 'Leave your present address with us,' sighs the bland clerk, opening the door.

QUOTAS

'Now,' says the Recorder in angelic tones,
'You have a right to four square metres of verse,
And since you write prose as well –
How you distinguish one from t'other is up to you –
Ten square metres of prose...

'These days scribblers live to quite an age,
There are poets around in plenty
And a positive plethora of prosers.
Hence in harmony with the spirit of the times
You must all of you share and share alike...

'Most of you are alike in any case...

'So I have spelt out your statutory rights,
And I leave it to your conscience,
And that, so to speak, of editors and publishers,
To see that you don't exceed your brief...

'If it isn't already too late,' the Recorder adds
Urbanely. 'Never too late to amend, they say.'

VANDALISM

Since the object in question is a modern poem,
A police spokesman stated yesterday,
It is hard to tell whether it has been damaged
Or not, or how badly.

Summoned to the scene, officers were uncertain
As to whether the work had been turned upside down
Or kcab ot tnorf
Or whether parts of it were [missing]

A doctor of letters has been called in
Together with experts on scansion and crosswords.
It appears to have been a short poem to begin with
So we hope to conclude our inquiries before long.

CONFESSION

In my youth I rarely used a dictionary
Except to search for words that sounded dirty.
In middle age I checked on spellings that were tricky.
Now, for every dozen words I use I look up thirty.

HARD TIMES FOR THE BLURB WRITER

We have little hesitation in claiming that
This relatively new book by XYZ is an
Advance on the author' previous one,
Which even so received favourable mention
In a prominent provincial newspaper.
The present work is well written in a style
Which combines the gritty with the fluid.
Less a novel than an extended documentary
Prose-poem, it is not simply the story of a
Man and a woman having an affair, but an account
Of good and evil in a contemporary setting and
All of us both men and women. 'The Spenser
Of Trollopes' is how the *Tipperary Reporter*
Has described Mr. Z. All in all we believe this
To be an interesting book by one of the more
Promising of living middle-aged authors.

READING PROOFS

Computers that correct your spelling! Would they could correct your sentiments. Would they could turn your dull roman days into lively italics. Would they could delete sick repetitions, expunge sad passages, supply omissions, enlarge virtues, reduce vices, justify your hopes. Would they could cancel memories, restore remembrances. If only, like a more merciful God, they could lose you for ever, painlessly, swiftly, without fuss.

DONOR

The heart has gone pit-a-pat once too often;
      bits seem to have fallen off.
No one would make great claims for the lungs.
The liver is well preserved, in alcohol.
The kidneys have made their presence felt.
The cornea has seen what it shouldn't have.
The brain, as you note, is in middling condition,
Second-hand car dealers would say it has a few thousand
      miles left in it.

The soul will presumably have flown.
At the best of times it was hard to locate.
You are unlikely to want it.

There is a chance of pre-emption by spontaneous
      combustion,
Very slight of course.
But a hot flush is already appearing.

WATCH

The second hand is advancing
Relentlessly (the obvious adverb
And since the watch has a new battery
So it ought to be)
One could calculate actuarially
The number of seconds left to one
Distinctly this side of the innumerable.

The other hands being less alarming
The second hand should be consulted
Only to make sure the watch is working –
Just as you still are
Which (by the way) is why you wanted
To know the hour.

SADNESS OF CARS

One after another, cries of alarm
Arise from the parked motors.
Abandoned by mummies and daddies
They are hungry and thirsty.
They have a pain in their innards.
They need to go to the garage.
They would like to visit the seaside.

One of them squawks, then another.
How can you ignore their misery?
Go out and pour oil for them.
Gaze into their hubcaps.
Pat them on their bonnets.
Fondle their bumpers.
Ring the Royal Society for the Prevention
   Of Cruelty to Automobiles.

Or boot them up their exhausts.
What are they wailing about?
Casual killers of children
Slayers of the old and slow
Big metal boxes inflamed by pygmies.

THE EMPEROR STRIKES BACK

The Emperor could see quite clearly
That the little boy was wearing clothes,
Though rather old ones.

How many little boys were there in the Empire?
The Chief Minister offered a rough estimate,
Most of them wearing rather old clothes.

There was a certain dignity in going naked
On special occasions,
But old clothes were a national disgrace.

'Hear, hear!' chorused the councillors.
The old clothes couldn't easily be disposed of,
The little boys on the other hand –

The question of little girls was deferred
Till the next convocation of the Imperial Council.

TREES - AFTER A KOREAN POEM

From time to time I gaze at the trees outside.
Yesterday I gazed at the trees outside.
Tomorrow no doubt I shall gaze at the trees.
This I did last year, this I shall do next year.

The trees are reasonably beautiful to view.
Also, it strikes me as I stroke my beard,
The trees can really be rather boring.

At this point the poet (incautiously absorbed
In the joys of wordplay) was set on by a band
Of seeming brigands emerging from the trees.
In truth their intent was solely to rid the world
Of useless unproductive lives, of drones
Who neither sowed nor reaped. These included
Scholars with long beards and high hats.

The story shows how one can never be sure.
Even the trees outside need to be heeded.

TREES – AFTER A WANDSWORTHIAN POEM

I peer at the trees outside
This is my present labour
I am looking for a parrot
Lost by a grieving neighbour.

Alas the parrot is green
(Which is all I know of the parrot)
And all the trees too are green
(Indeed they are all too green).

Though I long to be its saviour
However hard I have tried
The parrot is not to be seen
As I peer at the trees outside.

HELP ME

Dear Jane There is something wrong with me and I am so frightened Can you advise me I was watching the telly It was a comedy and people were laughing There was a girl who mislaid her Pills in a safety deposit and thought she was pregnant And everybody laughed but I didnt She was going to have an abortion but then her you know started and her boyfriend fell about And the people watching all laughed too And a young fellow with punk hair was angry and shouting because he had had a bad days mugging I wanted to laugh too but I couldnt Then his friend rushed to the toilet because he hadnt found a phone box to do it in And everybody laughed and laughed Except me I dont know why it is Am I going mad Im not like other people I feel so lonely I sit in front of the telly and cry Please help me Jane

MR P'S PASSPORT

Mr P lives in an airport lounge,
With excellent toilet facilities.
He is not allowed to starve.
Muzak floats by on a gentle breeze.

Quite a good class of neighbours too,
Though always changing.
Not always easy to sleep, though,
So much coming and going.

At times Mr P thinks of going himself.
He gets on a plane with a change of clothing
And arrives in another airport lounge.
Instead of Muzak there are fans on the ceiling,
In other ways there is little change.

An airport lounge is no man's land,
But for Mr P it is home.
Perhaps he will publish a memoir:
Some Airport Lounges I Have Known,
By 'A Citizen of the British Empire'.

SCENES

In the midst of common criminals,
A political prisoner, cleanshaven, pallid
And thin, the light of intelligence in his eyes...

In the midst of convicted terrorists,
A common criminal, dark-jowled, ruddy
And squat, the light of normality in his eyes...

HEARTS

He is a hard man, he brooks no opposition
His will shall be done.
His creatures rush to implement it
(More thoroughly at times than he intended).
They read his mind, so they reckon
For their eyes are sharp.
In their hearts they may not favour
Everything they do
(In private they wring their hands faintly)
But they do it.

How he must despise his creatures!
Us he must surely respect, we are honest
We are men of conviction, like him,
If of different convictions.
He must surely admire the likes of us
In his heart of hearts...

Don't bank on those hearts of hearts
My friends. They lie buried very deep.

WILLOW PATTERN

Birds gave the lovers no trouble at all,
At least the birds gave no trouble.

But now the lovers have turned to birds,
And birds – but the tale goes no further...

And why push events to their 'bitter end'?
Better to leave them to find out their own –

Just like the others, the birds and the lovers,
The troubles, and even the readers.

While the sky goes on, with angels and birds,
And the earth with its goblins and lovers.

A GOOD WORD

Nacreous is a good word. We must make a poem
Around it, or to one side, or behind it.
Nacreous. Not some drab anecdote of oysters.
No, something richer in human interest –

The nacreous face of a leper seen in Asia,
Stood up stern in the back of a trishaw,
Arched over the driver, the driver bent over
The handlebars and pumping away at the pedals.

A sight to remember, far rarer than pearls!
In the centre of town, in a public transport,
A towering leper: and a terrified driver,
Streaking through traffic, tin can at his tail.

– Or it is a chariot hurrying nearer?
A different driver. Inviting us in.
There's scant time left for poems, and we don't like
This one. A pity we ever stopped for nacreous.

— Massa, if God him numma-one big feller, all time have power, why he not kill Debbil so no more wickeds on this world here, no more lead stray like you say, make head huntings and cann'balism?

— God's gift, you must understand, the precious gift of free will –

— Me sabbee gift, no sabbee free wheel, me ign'ant sabbage –

— In his mercy God grants us the ever-present opportunity to forsake our evil ways. To put it in simple language, at any moment in our lifetime we are free to repent and turn over a new leaf. And so it is even with the Devil.

— But this Debbil you tell live for plenty time, Massa. He no need act good for long long time coming, all stretch between he do more bad thing. Better God say him, Me boss feller, you not be everlasting no more, and God chop off Debbil his head 'fore say Jack Rob'son, not wait Debbil be more big and strong bime-by.

— Isn't it time you started to roast that kid – that young goat? Which I shot expressly to prove that it tastes quite as delicious as human flesh does, or so you say, and is acceptable to God as well.

— But me called Friday, near end of week, not have all

time wait for Debbil be nice, kind, turn over new leaves. Me t'ink eat young kiddie goat pronto, nebber mind roast on pesky fire, burn flesh of human finger. And mebbe God smell and want accept too. Chop chop.

FAUST GREETED

Of course in the more recent versions you had
To be saved - saved from *what doesn't exist*
Of course. Freed on some technicality, or left
Among the living to set a suitable example,
Or else to suffer *the hell that we all suffer* -
Toothache or sex or spots or lack of cash.

This, you now perceive, is not a modern story.
The *inconceivable* is perfectly conceived,
Even familiar, no truck with novelties in hell -
Thanks to your busy scribblers, whose metaphors
We happily adopt au pied de la lettre.

So the old polarities. Freezing, then burning;
Starving, then force-fed like a Strasbourg goose;
Alone all all alone, then one of huddled trillions,
No room to pick the famous maggot from your eye;
Disgraced in all men's eyes and headlines, then
Never heard of, never seen on television.
Progress, you know, has need of contraries.

Worst of all is not to see the face of God?
You must be joking. Worst of all for you would be
To see it. He's an infrequent visitor, luckily,
Once in a blue moon, glimpsed through smoked glasses.

Your cup runneth over; no one takes it from you.
Hell is lots of other people. Someone isn't married
And that's his pain; another is: that's his. Then
They swap sides. Hell is a city filthier than London.

41

All your own growing. I only sowed the seed.
When man lay in his cradle gurgling, there came
A wicked fairy. Imagination was the gift I brought.

THE SYSTEM

The damned stand over here and watch the blessed
Being happy: this makes them damnably wretched.
The blessed sit over there and watch the damned
Being wretched: this makes them blessedly happy.

These know they are miserable because the others
Are obviously joyful; those know they are joyful
Because the others are unmistakably miserable.
So far the system has proved quite satisfactory.

There seems no reason why it shouldn't work
For ever. Punishments would pall pretty quickly
(There's a lot of time to pall in eternity),
Rewards would lose their charm. Then how to tell
Which lot was which?: two shades of apathy.
But God, who knows all, knew this. What is simplest
Lasts longest: the secret of perpetual emotion.

A HAPPIER ENDING TO GREAT EXPECTATIONS

Yes, I know, you are the author
Of course, and I'm only a reader
As we say in the trade, or copy-editor.

But we wonder if you could see your way
To tempering the conclusion?
One really ought to think of the public
(Who on this occasion, to add to the confusion,
Are also the characters).
They don't much like endings to be the end.

One might have expected some such story-line
Had an enemy written it instead of a friend.

What I have written I have written –
I don't wish to sound like a philistine
But that was a man who wrote what he wrote
In Hebrew and Greek and Latin,
What little he wrote, that Roman.

This is the writing that was written –
It was, but like what we call graffiti,
The writing in question was inscribed on a wall
And referred to the Medes and Persians uniquely.

What you have written you can always rewrite,
Just a little brighter.
Let your heart indite a good matter,
Your pen is the pen of a ready writer.
Let your good heart take a turn for the better.

IT'S YOUR OWN FAULT

Of course you can play with them.
There's no harm in them.
They are only words.
Words alone are certain good, said someone.
And someone else said:
Unlike sticks and stones
Words will never break your bones.

(That is called a rhyme. A rhyme
Is nice to play with too from time to time.)
What? They've turned nasty?
They've clawed you and bitten you?
Dear me, there's blood all over the place,
And broken bones.

They were perfectly tame when I left.
Something they ate must have disagreed with them.
You mean you fed them on *meaning*?
No wonder then.

HAIKU

Gaspings and gulpings –
poetic equivalent
of emphysema.

AND SMALLER IS BEAUTIFULLER

Shorter than haiku
by one syllable: the min-
imalist po

CONTINUED

-em for all things end
saving present company
to be continued.

ON SOME TRANSLATIONS
BY HELMUT WINTER

Reading them against the old originals –
Back then, you think, you had some talent,
Almost lyrical, a gentle sadness,
Here and there a word not quite expected,
And now and then some simple humour...
Ah well, sadness comes expensive these days,
The unexpected takes too large a toll,
Nothing's simple enough for simple humour,
While lyricism faded long ago...
What's left? These phrases in a foreign tongue.

J.R.R. Tolkien
The Books, The Films, The Whole Cultural Phenomenon

by Jeremy Mark Robinson

A new critical study of J.R.R. Tolkien, creator of Middle-earth and author of *The Lord of the Rings, The Hobbit* and *The Silmarillion*, among other books.
This new critical study explores Tolkien's major writings (*The Lord of the Rings, The Hobbit, Beowulf: The Monster and the Critics, The Letters, The Silmarillion* and *The History of Middle-earth* volumes); Tolkien and fairy tales; the mythological, political and religious aspects of Tolkien's Middle-earth; the critics' response to Tolkien's fiction over the decades; the Tolkien industry (merchandizing, toys, role-playing games, posters, Tolkien societies, conferences and the like); Tolkien in visual and fantasy art; the cultural aspects of The Lord of the Rings (from the 1950s to the present); Tolkien's fiction's relationship with other fantasy fiction, such as C.S. Lewis and *Harry Potter*; and the TV, radio and film versions of Tolkien's books, including the 2001-03 Hollywood interpretations of *The Lord of the Rings*.
This new book draws on contemporary cultural theory and analysis and offers a sympathetic and illuminating (and sceptical) account of the Tolkien phenomenon. This book is designed to appeal to the general reader (and viewer) of Tolkien: it is written in a clear, jargon-free and easily-accessible style.

754pp   ISBN 1-86171-057-7   £25.00 / $37.50

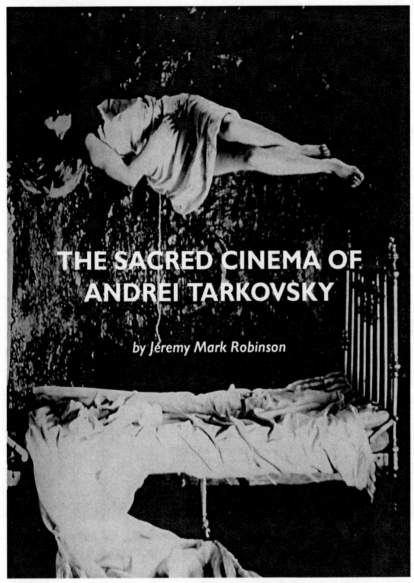

THE SACRED CINEMA OF ANDREI TARKOVSKY

by Jeremy Mark Robinson

A new study of the Russian filmmaker Andrei Tarkovsky (1932-1986), director of seven feature films, including *Andrei Roublyov, Mirror, Solaris, Stalker* and *The Sacrifice*.
This is one of the most comprehensive and detailed studies of Tarkovsky's cinema available. Every film is explored in depth, with scene-by-scene analyses. All aspects of Tarkovsky's output are critiqued, including editing, camera, staging, script, budget, collaborations, production, sound, music, performance and spirituality. Tarkovsky is placed with a European New Wave tradition of filmmaking, alongside directors like Ingmar Bergman, Carl Theodor Dreyer, Pier Paolo Pasolini and Robert Bresson.
An essential addition to film studies.

Illustrations: 150 b/w, 4 colour. 682 pages. First edition. Hardback.

Publisher: Crescent Moon Publishing. Distributor: Gardners Books.

ISBN 1-86171-096-8 (9781861710963) £60.00 / $105.00

The Best of Peter Redgrove's Poetry
The Book of Wonders

by Peter Redgrove, edited and introduced by Jeremy Robinson

Poems of wet shirts and 'wonder-awakening dresses'; honey, wasps and bees; orchards and apples; rivers, seas and tides; storms, rain, weather and clouds; waterworks; labyrinths; amazing perfumes; the Cornish landscape (Penzance, Perranporth, Falmouth, Boscastle, the Lizard and Scilly Isles); the sixth sense and 'extra-sensuous perception'; witchcraft; alchemical vessels and laboratories; yoga; menstruation; mines, minerals and stones; sand dunes; mud-baths; mythology; dreaming; vulvas; and lots of sex magic. This book gathers together poetry (and prose) from every stage of Redgrove's career, and every book. It includes pieces that have only appeared in small presses and magazines, and in uncollected form.

'Peter Redgrove is really an extraordinary poet' (George Szirtes, *Quarto* magazine) 'Peter Redgrove is one of the few significant poets now writing... His 'means' are indeed brilliant and delightful. Technically he is a poet essentially of brilliant and unexpected images...he never disappoints' (Kathleen Raine, *Temenos* magazine).

240pp   ISBN 1-86171-063-1   2nd edition   £19.99 / $29.50

Sex–Magic–Poetry–Cornwall
A Flood of Poems

by Peter Redgrove. Edited with an essay by Jeremy Robinson

A marvellous collection of poems by one of Britain's best but underrated poets, Peter Redgrove. This book brings together some of Redgrove's wildest and most passionate works, creating a 'flood' of poetry. Philip Hobsbaum called Redgrove 'the great poet of our time', while Angela Carter said: 'Redgrove's language can light up a page.' Redgrove ranks alongside Ted Hughes and Sylvia Plath. He is in every way a 'major poet'. Robinson's essay analyzes all of Redgrove's poetic work, including his use of sex magic, natural science, menstruation, psychology, myth, alchemy and feminism.
A new edition, including a new introduction, new preface and new bibliography.

'Robinson's enthusiasm is winning, and his perceptive readings are supported by a very useful bibliography' (*Acumen* magazine)
'*Sex-Magic-Poetry-Cornwall* is a very rich essay... It is like a brightly-lighted box. (Peter Redgrove)
'This is an excellent selection of poetry and an extensive essay on the themes and theories of this unusual poet by Jeremy Robinson' (*Chapman* magazine)

220pp   New, 3rd edition   ISBN 1-86171-070-4   £14.99 / $23.50

THE ART OF
ANDY GOLDSWORTHY

COMPLETE WORKS: SPECIAL EDITION
(PAPERBACK and HARDBACK)

by William Malpas

A new, special edition of the study of the contemporary British sculptor, Andy Goldsworthy, including a new introduction, new bibliography and many new illustrations.

This is the most comprehensive, up-to-date, well-researched and in-depth account of Goldsworthy's art available anywhere.

Andy Goldsworthy makes land art. His sculpture is a sensitive, intuitive response to nature, light, time, growth, the seasons and the earth. Goldsworthy's environmental art is becoming ever more popular: 1993's art book *Stone* was a bestseller; the press raved about Goldsworthy taking over a number of London West End art galleries in 1994; during 1995 Goldsworthy designed a set of Royal Mail stamps and had a show at the British Museum. Malpas surveys all of Goldsworthy's art, and analyzes his relation with other land artists such as Robert Smithson, Walter de Maria, Richard Long and David Nash, and his place in the contemporary British art scene.

The Art of Andy Goldsworthy discusses all of Goldsworthy's important and recent exhibitions and books, including the *Sheepfolds* project; the TV documentaries; *Wood* (1996); the New York Holocaust memorial (2003); and Goldsworthy's collaboration on a dance performance.

Illustrations: 70 b/w, 1 colour. 330 pages. New, special, 2nd edition.
Publisher: Crescent Moon Publishing. Distributor: Gardners Books.

ISBN 1-86171-059-3 (9781861710598) (Paperback) £25.00 / $44.00

ISBN 1-86171-080-1 (9781861710802) (Hardback) £60.00 / $105.00

CRESCENT MOON PUBLISHING

ARTS, PAINTING, SCULPTURE

The Art of Andy Goldsworthy: Complete Works(Pbk)
The Art of Andy Goldsworthy: Complete Works (Hbk)
Andy Goldsworthy in Close-Up (Pbk)
Andy Goldsworthy in Close-Up (Hbk)
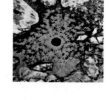
Land Art: A Complete Guide
Richard Long: The Art of Walking
The Art of Richard Long: Complete Works (Pbk)
The Art of Richard Long: Complete Works (Hbk)
Richard Long in Close-Up

Land Art In the UK
Land Art in Close-Up
Installation Art in Close-Up
Minimal Art and Artists In the 1960s and After

Colourfield Painting
Land Art DVD, TV documentary
Andy Goldsworthy DVD, TV documentary
The Erotic Object: Sexuality in Sculpture From Prehistory to the Present Day
Sex in Art: Pornography and Pleasure in Painting and Sculpture
Postwar Art
Sacred Gardens: The Garden in Myth, Religion and Art
Glorification: Religious Abstraction in Renaissance and 20th Century Art
Early Netherlandish Painting
Leonardo da Vinci
Piero della Francesca

Giovanni Bellini
Fra Angelico: Art and Religion in the Renaissance
Mark Rothko: The Art of Transcendence

Frank Stella: American Abstract Artist
Jasper Johns: Painting By Numbers
Brice Marden

Alison Wilding: The Embrace of Sculpture
Vincent van Gogh: Visionary Landscapes
Eric Gill: Nuptials of God
Constantin Brancusi: Sculpting the Essence of Things
Max Beckmann
Egon Schiele: Sex and Death In Purple Stockings
Delizioso Fotografico Fervore: Works In Process 1
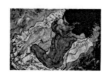
Sacro Cuore: Works In Process 2
The Light Eternal: J.M.W. Turner
The Madonna Glorified: Karen Arthurs

LITERATURE

J.R.R. Tolkien: The Books, The Films, The Whole Cultural Phenomenon
Harry Potter
Sexing Hardy: Thomas Hardy and Feminism
Thomas Hardy's *Tess of the d'Urbervilles*
Thomas Hardy's *Jude the Obscure*
Thomas Hardy: The Tragic Novels
Love and Tragedy: Thomas Hardy
The Poetry of Landscape in Hardy
Wessex Revisited: Thomas Hardy and John Cowper Powys
Wolfgang Iser: Essays
Petrarch, Dante and the Troubadours
Maurice Sendak and the Art of Children's Book Illustration
Andrea Dworkin
Cixous, Irigaray, Kristeva: The *Jouissance* of French Feminism
Julia Kristeva: Art, Love, Melancholy, Philosophy, Semiotics and Psychoanalysis
Hélene Cixous I Love You: The *Jouissance* of Writing
Luce Irigaray: Lips, Kissing, and the Politics of Sexual Difference
Peter Redgrove: Here Comes the Flood
Peter Redgrove: Sex-Magic-Poetry-Cornwall
Lawrence Durrell: Between Love and Death, East and West
Love, Culture & Poetry: Lawrence Durrell
Cavafy: Anatomy of a Soul
German Romantic Poetry: Goethe, Novalis, Heine, Hölderlin, Schlegel, Schiller
Feminism and Shakespeare
Shakespeare: Selected Sonnets
Shakespeare: Love, Poetry & Magic
The Passion of D.H. Lawrence
D.H. Lawrence: Symbolic Landscapes
D.H. Lawrence: Infinite Sensual Violence
Rimbaud: Arthur Rimbaud and the Magic of Poetry
The Ecstasies of John Cowper Powys
Sensualism and Mythology: The Wessex Novels of John Cowper Powys
Amorous Life: John Cowper Powys and the Manifestation of Affectivity (H.W. Fawkner)
Postmodern Powys: New Essays on John Cowper Powys (Joe Boulter)
Rethinking Powys: Critical Essays on John Cowper Powys
Paul Bowles & Bernardo Bertolucci
Rainer Maria Rilke
In the Dim Void: Samuel Beckett
Samuel Beckett Goes into the Silence
André Gide: Fiction and Fervour
Jackie Collins and the Blockbuster Novel
Blinded By Her Light: The Love-Poetry of Robert Graves
The Passion of Colours: Travels In Mediterranean Lands
Poetic Forms
The Dolphin-Boy

POETRY

The Best of Peter Redgrove's Poetry
Peter Redgrove: Here Comes The Flood
Peter Redgrove: Sex-Magic-Poetry-Cornwall
Ursula Le Guin: Walking In Cornwall
Dante: Selections From the Vita Nuova
Petrarch, Dante and the Troubadours
William Shakespeare: Selected Sonnets
Blinded By Her Light: The Love-Poetry of Robert Graves
Emily Dickinson: Selected Poems
Emily Brontë: Poems
Thomas Hardy: Selected Poems
Percy Bysshe Shelley: Poems
John Keats: Selected Poems
D.H. Lawrence: Selected Poems
Edmund Spenser: Poems
John Donne: Poems
Henry Vaughan: Poems
Sir Thomas Wyatt: Poems
Robert Herrick: Selected Poems
Rilke: Space, Essence and Angels in the Poetry of Rainer Maria Rilke
Rainer Maria Rilke: Selected Poems
Friedrich Hölderlin: Selected Poems
Arseny Tarkovsky: Selected Poems
Arthur Rimbaud: Selected Poems
Arthur Rimbaud: A Season in Hell
Arthur Rimbaud and the Magic of Poetry
D.J. Enright: By-Blows
Jeremy Reed: Brigitte's Blue Heart
Jeremy Reed: Claudia Schiffer's Red Shoes
Gorgeous Little Orpheus
Radiance: New Poems
Crescent Moon Book of Nature Poetry
Crescent Moon Book of Love Poetry
Crescent Moon Book of Mystical Poetry
Crescent Moon Book of Elizabethan Love Poetry
Crescent Moon Book of Metaphysical Poetry
Crescent Moon Book of Romantic Poetry
Pagan America: New American Poetry

MEDIA, CINEMA, FEMINISM and CULTURAL STUDIES

J.R.R. Tolkien: The Books, The Films, The Whole Cultural Phenomenon
Harry Potter
Cixous, Irigaray, Kristeva: The *Jouissance* of French Feminism
Julia Kristeva: Art, Love, Melancholy, Philosophy, Semiotics and   Psychoanalysis
Luce Irigaray: Lips, Kissing, and the Politics of Sexual Difference
Hélene Cixous I Love You: The *Jouissance* of Writing
Andrea Dworkin
'Cosmo Woman': The World of Women's Magazines
Women in Pop Music
Discovering the Goddess (Geoffrey Ashe)
The Poetry of Cinema
The Sacred Cinema of Andrei Tarkovsky (Pbk and Hbk)
Paul Bowles & Bernardo Bertolucci
Media Hell: Radio, TV and the Press
An Open Letter to the BBC
Detonation Britain: Nuclear War in the UK
Feminism and Shakespeare
Wild Zones: Pornography, Art and Feminism
Sex in Art: Pornography and Pleasure in Painting and Sculpture
Sexing Hardy: Thomas Hardy and Feminism

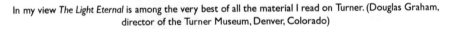

In my view *The Light Eternal* is among the very best of all the material I read on Turner. (Douglas Graham, director of the Turner Museum, Denver, Colorado)

The Light Eternal is a model monograph, an exemplary job. The subject matter of the book is beautifully organised and dead on beam. (Lawrence Durrell)

It is amazing for me to see my work treated with such passion and respect. (Andrea Dworkin)

Sex-Magic-Poetry-Cornwall is a very rich essay... It is like a brightly-lighted box. (Peter Redgrove)

CRESCENT MOON PUBLISHING
P.O. Box 393, Maidstone, Kent, ME14 5XU, United Kingdom.
01622-729593 (UK) 01144-1622-729593 (US) 0044-1622-729593 (other territories)
cresmopub@yahoo.co.uk   www.crescentmoon.org.uk

Printed in the United Kingdom by
Lightning Source UK Ltd., Milton Keynes
141648UK00002B/18/P